AIRCRAFT OF WORLD WAR II

JADE BOOKS

Distributed by Omega Books
1 West Street, Ware
Hertfordshire

ISBN 0 907853 57 9

Printed in Hong Kong

CONTENTS

Fighters and Attack Aircraft

The Gladiator was designed by H P 'Harry' Folland as a private venture, intended as a refined successor to the Gloster Gauntlet which, with the Bristol Bulldog, formed the nucleus of Britain's fighter force in the mid-thirties. The Gladiator prototype first flew on 12 September 1934 in the hands of Gloster's legendary test pilot Gerry Sayer.

The Gladiator was outdated before it entered production, and was slower than some bombers then projected, but an Air Ministry order was placed in June 1935 for 23 aircraft as a stop-gap while the more advanced monoplane fighters were being developed, and was followed by another contract for 180 three months later. Final orders totalled 480 for the RAF, 60 Sea Gladiators for the Fleet Air Arm and 216 for export.

The first Gladiators entered service with 72 Squadron at RAF Tangmere, Sussex, in February 1937, and equipped nine squadrons by September that year. They were a delight to fly, perhaps second only to the Hawker Fury in handling, though forward visibility between the cabane struts was poor and the accommodation was only marginally more cosy than that of its open-cockpit contemporaries, for there was no heating and at altitude the windscreen frosted over. Armament consisted of two Vickers and two Lewis guns on the first 70 aircraft, and a quartet of Brownings on later machines, one each side of the forward fuselage synchronised to fire through the propeller arc and one beneath each lower wing in a streamlined blister fairing.

In all, 25 RAF squadrons received Gladiators and 13 squadrons still had them when war broke out, though they had largely been replaced in front-line operations by Spitfires and Hurricanes. But it was the old Gladiator, anachronism though it was, which intercepted the first Luftwaffe raiders over the Firth of Forth in September 1939, and on 17 October 1939 three pilots from B Flight, 607 Squadron, successfully attacked a Dornier Do 18 flying-boat and forced it to land off the Northumberland coast.

Top right: The Fiat CR.42 may be regarded as the ultimate biplane fighter, first flying in 1939 and resulting from Italy's experience in the Spanish Civil War. Agile and strong, the CR.42 could reach 267 mph (430 km/h) on 840 hp (627 kW), compared with the P-26's 234 mph (377 km/h) on 550 hp (410 kW), but contemporary monoplanes of cantilever construction and fitted with retractable landing gear could surpass 350 mph (563 km/h).

Below right: A contemporary of the P-36, the Seversky P-35 was also built in small numbers and served usefully in introducing US Army Air Corps pilots to the modern monoplane fighter.

Below: The Shuttleworth Trust's unique airworthy Gloster Gladiator touches down at Old Warden.

With a two-blade wooden Watts propeller, the Gladiator's top speed was 248 mph. Its rate of climb, 2,300 ft per minute, was much the same as the Gauntlet's, but it was a better handling machine, some say second only to the Hawker Fury, though forward visibility between the cabane struts was poor and despite the enclosed canopy the lack of any cockpit heating made high altitude flying a misery.

Above: The Curtiss P-40 Warhawk was the first mass-produced US single-seat fighter and with the Bell P-39 formed the basic USAAF fighter strength during the early war years; it was also supplied in bulk to other Allied air forces including the Russian. The one pictured flies from the CAF field at Harlingen and demonstrates the suitability of the P-40's frontal shape for fearsome decoration.

Right: Among the first fruits of the epoch-making Mikoyan-Gurevich collaboration was the MiG-3 fighter. Seen here is a squadron of MiG-3s on duty in 1942. Although compact and fast, early MiG fighters were not particularly successful and the 3,000 or so built were largely relegated to reconnaissance duties by the end of 1943, giving no hint of the fame to come.

Curtiss P-40

Country of origin: USA.

Crew: 1.

Dimensions: Wingspan 11.38 m (37 ft 4 in); length (radial) 8.73 m (28 ft 7¾ in).

Weights: Empty 2060 kg (4,541 lb); maximum loaded 3022 kg (6,662 lb).

Engine: P-36, Hawk 75: either Wright R-1820 Cyclone, usually of 1,200 hp, or Pratt & Whitney R-1830 Twin Wasp of 1,050–1,200 hp.

Maximum speed: Typically 520 km/h (323 mph).

Service ceiling: All versions 10050 m (33,000 ft).

Range: All versions, without drop tank, 1130 km (700 miles).

Military load: P-36: one 12.7 mm (0.5 in) and one or three 7.62 mm (0.30 in) Browning machine guns; **Hawk 75A:** six 7.5 mm or (RAF) 7.7 mm (0.303 in); **Tomahawks:** six 7.7 mm (0.303 in); (later versions) six 12.7 mm (0.5 in) plus fuselage rack for bomb or tank of 272 kg (600 lb) and wing racks for two 227 kg (500 lb).

Above: A Curtiss P-36A sports extemporised camouflage for US Army manoeuvres. The first 'modern' low-wing monoplane fighter to come from Curtiss, the P-36 series was not produced in large numbers, but proved itself an effective bridge between the interim P-26 and fully fledged monoplanes such as the Bell P-39 and Curtiss P-40.

Below: The Mitsubishi A5M was the Imperial Japanese Navy's first monoplane fighter, and a classic of its type. Though it retained fixed landing gear and an open cockpit, the 'Claude' – as it was coded by the Allies in World War 2, had a cantilever wing and metal construction, offering most of the biplane's agility with some of the monoplane's performance.

The Yak-3, which appeared in December 1942, was essentially the Yak-1M optimised for high-altitude combat, the Russians having realised that although the decisive air battle might be fought at low and medium altitudes, the high altitudes could not merely be given to the Germans for trouble-free reconnaissance and the like. The Yakovlev bureau at first wanted the more modern Klimov M-107 for the Yak-3, but on Stalin's personal dictate this was refused, the Yak-3 thus appearing with improved versions of the M-105, culminating in the VK-105PF-2 which developed 1,290 hp (962 kW) for take-off. The Yak-3 entered service in mid-1943, and soon built for itself an awesome reputation: at 10,825 ft (3,300 m) the Yak-3 was some 25 mph (40 km/h) faster than the Bf 109G, and at low altitude it could out-turn the Fw 190 with ease. However, at altitudes above 19,685 ft (6,000 m) the German fighters were still superior. Further improvements were effected in the Yak-3U, which finally received the 1,700-hp

Right: The Russian philosophy so far as fighters were concerned was one of simplicity: volume production of only a few variants of the right fighter types, which had to be easy to build and to maintain, have powerful armament, and excel in the low- and medium-altitude arenas considered paramount by the Red Air Force. One of the best examples of this philosophy was the Yakovlev Yak-3, this example being brought to France by the 'Normandie-Niemen' squadron in 1945.

(1,268-kW) VK-107A and differed from the basic Yak-3 in having an all-metal structure and the impressive armament of one motor-mounted 37 mm cannon and two fuselage-mounted 20 mm cannon. With a maximum speed of 447 mph (720 km/h) at 18,865 ft (5,750 m), the Yak-3U was a formidable fighter right up to the end of the war.

Below: The blocky appearance that had characterised French aircraft of the 1930s disappeared entirely with the svelte Dewoitine D.520 single-seat fighter. This type, which entered service in 1939, was in most ways comparable with the best British and German fighters.

From 1941 the Hurricane served mainly overseas, including the Soviet Union. It was the obvious choice for conversion into a carrier-based fighter, and was chosen for the CAM (catapult-armed merchantman) ships which gave great assistance to the harassed convoys.

Top left: A crude aircraft by comparison with contemporary Western aircraft, the Yakovlev Yak-1M was nevertheless a highly effective fighter, well suited to the difficult climatic conditions and primitive airfields of the Eastern Front, and of more than holding its own in low-level combat with German fighters. Note the pilot's excellent fields of vision.

Left: Yakovlev Yak-7B fighters, looking slightly odd in their factory-fresh paint, await delivery to Red Air Force units. This variant was evolved from the Yak-7V two-seat conversion trainer and Yak-7A single-seater, and was distinguishable from the Yak-1 most easily by the position of its radiator, which was moved forward to a position under the front of the cockpit in the Yak-7 series.

Lower left: Counterpart of the Yak-3 (itself a modification of the Yak-1M) from the other branch of the basic Yak-1 series, the Yakovlev Yak-9 was slightly larger and used metal spars in its wing structure. Seen here are Yak-9DD long-range escort fighters, produced specifically for the support of the Yugoslav communist partisans under Tito.

Left: The Ki-61 Hien (Swallow) was odd-man-out in Japanese fighters in having a liquid-cooled engine, and was probably more dangerous to the Allies in the early encounters for that reason. Codenamed 'Tony' and used as a light bomber, the Hien started to appear with Japanese squadrons in the second half of 1942 and total deliveries were more than 2,700.

Hawker Hurricane

Country of origin: Great Britain.

Crew: 1.

Dimensions: Wingspan 12.192 m (40 ft 0 in); length, **Mk I:** 9.55 m (31 ft 5 in), later: 9.81 m (32 ft 2½ in); wing area 23.97 m² (257.5 ft²).

Weights: Empty, **I:** 2260 kg (4,982 lb), **IIC:** 2566 kg (5,657 lb); maximum loaded, **I:** 3397 kg (7,490 lb), **IIC:** 3742 kg (8,250 lb), **IV:** 3856 kg (8,500 lb).

Engine: Rolls-Royce Merlin vee-12 liquid-cooled; **I:** Merlin III, 1,030 hp; **II:** Merlin XX, 1,280 hp; **IV:** Merlin 24 or 27, 1,620 hp; Canadian **MK X, XI, XII:** Packard V-1650-1, 1,300 hp (Merlin 28, 29).

Maximum speed: I: 519 km/h (322 mph), later: typically 531 km/h (330 mph).

Service ceiling: All versions, approx. 10365 m (34,000 ft).

Range: I: 813 km (505 miles), **IIC:** without drop tanks 740 km (460 miles).

Pilots of No. 111 Squadron race to their Hawker Hurricanes during the battle for France, May 1940.

Military load: I: Eight 7.7 mm (0.303 in) Browning machine guns, each of 333 rounds; **Belgian I:** four 12.7 mm (0.5 in) FN-Browning; **IIA:** eight 7.7 mm (0.303 in) and two 227 kg (500 lb) bombs or drop tanks; **IIB:** 12 7.7 mm (0.303 in) and bombs; **IIC:** four 20 mm Hispano and bombs; **IID:** two 40 mm Vickers S, plus two 7.7 mm (0.303 in).

13

Above: It was standard practice in the Second World War to relegate obsolescent fighters to secondary theatres, where they could perform usefully until the enemy sent in some fully up-to-date aircraft. Such a fate befell the Hurricane, which was relegated as a fighter to North Africa, and then became a fighter-bomber in the second half of that campaign and in the Italian campaign.

Below: A Canadian-built Hurricane IIB preserved by the Strathallan Collection.

The Spitfire's task was primarily to fly top cover against the Luftwaffe's Messerschmitt escort fighters while the slower Hurricanes attacked the invading bombers. The Spitfire 1A was just marginally faster than a Bf 109E, and with greater wing area could turn more steeply and tightly if its pilot dared pull enough *g*. Most, used to slow unresponsive trainers, would back off under the unfamiliar and uncomfortable *g* loads, giving the advantage to the more-experienced Luftwaffe fliers. At altitudes above 20,000 feet the German fighter was superior, and could escape from a

Contrast in Spitfire wing forms —
Mitchell's pleasing ellipse of the Mark
IX, (*left*) privately owned and based at
Booker; and (*right*) the most widely
used clipped C wing of the Shuttleworth
Trust's Mark V.

Spitfire by pushing over into a
high-speed dive; the Bf 109E
had direct fuel injection,
whereas the Merlins in Spitfires
and Hurricanes were fed by
float carburettors. For all that,
Spitfires achieved remarkable
victories against formidable
odds. German ace Adolf
Galland, when asked by
Reichsmarschall Hermann
Göring what he most needed to
beat the RAF, allegedly replied
'a squadron of Spitfires'.

While the Polikarpov I-16 can be regarded as the bridge between the biplane and monoplane eras, the Supermarine Spitfire (inset) was definitely a classic example of the fully developed monoplane fighter, with an advanced engine, airframe reflecting the contemporary 'state of the art', enclosed cockpit, considerable protection and heavy firepower. Seen below are a pair of Spitfire Vs over the Allied beach-head at Anzio in Italy.

Below: The most significant of the early Bf 109s was the 'Emil' or Bf 109E, powered by the great DB 601 inline. This definitive mark had excellent performance, the ability to push straight down into a dive without a preliminary and time-consuming half-roll, and an armament that included both machine-guns and cannon. Though these latter were relatively slow-firing and of low muzzle-velocity (and so limited in range), they did pack a considerably heftier punch than the rifle-calibre machine-guns of British fighters.

There can be no doubt that Messerschmitt had produced a great aircraft, especially when the introduction of the DB 601 in the Bf 109E produced the first version that could stand up well to combat at all altitudes against the best opposition in the world. With its DB 601A developing 1,100 hp (821 kW) at 12,145 ft (3,700 m), the Bf 109E was capable of 354 mph (570 km/h) at 16,405 ft (5,000 m), could climb to 30,100 ft (9,175 m) and had an optimum climb rate of 2,990 ft (910 m) per minute at 13,125 ft (4,000 m). Armament comprised a pair of fuselage-mounted 7.92-mm (0.31-in) MG 17 machine-guns and two wing-mounted 20-mm MG FF cannon, or four machine-guns and one cannon, or four machine-guns. Armour for the pilot was provided, self-sealing fuel tanks reduced the risk of fire, and all in all the Bf 109E

was perhaps the best combat fighter in the world, with agility perhaps slightly less than that of the Supermarine Spitfire, but the enormously important ability to dive without a preliminary half-roll thanks to its fuel-injected rather than normally carburetted engine.

Above: The Ta 152C was the only variant of Kurt Tank's best fighter to enter service. Powered by a Daimler-Benz DB 603L inline with water-methanol boost, the type also served as the basis for the Ta 152H with the Jumo 213E/B inline provided with methanol-water and nitrous-oxide boost. Span was increased to 47 ft 5¾ in (14.50 m), the combination of power and wing area increasing service ceiling to a prodigious 48,560 ft (14,800 m). Maximum speed was 472 mph (760 km/h) at 41,010 ft (12,500 m) with nitrous-oxide boost.

Top left: The Messerschmitt Bf 110G-4 was the first variant of this *Zerstörer* (destroyer) sub-model to appear as a night-fighter, with FuG 212 Lichtenstein radar and an armament of four machine-guns and two 20 mm cannon.

Top right: The Focke-Wulf Fw 190 was undoubtedly one of the great fighters of all time, and perhaps the finest German fighter to enter widespread service in the Second World War.

Above: Seen at the Confederate Air Force's 'Rebel Field' at Harlingen, Texas, is a Hispano HA-1112 based on the Bf 109 but built in Spain during the early 1950s with a Rolls-Royce Merlin engine (a neat juxtaposition of wartime enemies). The 'German' markings include those of Jagdgeschwader 52 on the nose.

Right: Komet very-short-range interceptor powered by a rocket motor. It was built purely for home defence and sacrificed everything (even a very high proportion of its pilots' lives, as it turned out) to achieve a rate of climb of 30,000 ft in less than three minutes.

Below: The Messerschmitt Me 262 was a true portent of fighter developments in the later 1940s and early 1950s thanks to its advanced aerodynamics, jet engines and tricycle landing gear. This is an Me 262B-1a/U1 night-fighter.

The 262 was an enormous technical achievement, and the only turbojet fighter to have any influence on the war. The 262 was a beautiful machine to fly, but there were still problems, including basic engine unreliability and short life, formation flying was almost impossible because of engine-handling limitations, and there were also aiming problems.

On 25 March 1942 a flight was made with this aircraft fitted with two BMW003 turbojets; these promptly failed, and the piston engine just managed to bring the machine back to a landing. But on 18 July 1942 test-pilot Wendel made a perfect flight in the third prototype, fitted with the Junkers engine.

Left: The He 162 Salamander (or Volksjäger), the Luftwaffe's last fighter designed in a frantic last-ditch effort in the winter of 1944–45 and hurriedly put into production at a planned rate of 70 a day without factories.

Below: The first notable design of the re-formed Northrop Company in the early 1940's was the P-61 Black Widow, the world's first purpose-designed radar-equipped night fighter.

Messerschmitt Me 262

Country of origin: Germany.

Crew: 1, except B-series: 2.

Dimensions: Wingspan 12.48 m (40 ft 11½ in); length, **A-series:** 10.6 m (34 ft 9½ in), **B-series:** 11.8 m (38 ft 9 in); wing area 21.7 m² (234 ft²).

Range: A-1a, high altitude: 1050 km (650 miles).
Military load: A-1a: four 30 mm MK108 cannon; **A-1a/U1:** two 30 mm MK103, two MK108 and two 20 mm MG151; **A-1b:** as A-1a plus 24 spin-stabilized R4/M 50 mm rockets; **A-2a:** as A-1a plus two 250 kg (51 lb) bombs.

Maximum speed: A-1a: 866 km/h (538 mph); **A-2a,** with bombs: 750 km/h (466 mph).

Engines: Two Junkers Jumo 004B-1, -2 or -3 single-shaft axial-flow turbojets each rated at 900 kg (1,980 lb) static thrust.

Right: The Bell Airacobra failed in its intended role as an interceptor, but proved to be a potent low-level attack aircraft, its strength and stability allowing the heavy armament to be used to maximum effect. Seen here are P-39D Airacobras of the USAAF. This variant was developed to provide the type with self-sealing fuel tanks, which combat experience in Europe had shown to be absolutely essential.

Top right: The feature which most distinguished the Bell P-39 Airacobra in the air was its slim nose, made possible by the location of the engine aft of the pilot, from where it drove the propeller by means of an extension shaft. This powerplant configuration had been selected to improve manoeuvrability (by placing the heavy engine nearer the centre of gravity) and to leave the nose clear for a heavy forward-firing armament, including a 37 mm cannon.

26

Below, inset: Ranked No. 1 in numbers produced of US fighters was the Republic P-47 Thunderbolt. For a long time it was also the biggest and heaviest single-seat fighter, with an all-up weight of around eight tons in its main P-47D production form. Although the P-47 appeared fairly late in the war, making its first operational appearance in April 1943, no fewer than 15,660 were built for the USAF and RAF. The one illustrated is the final production mark P-47N, developed primarily for Pacific-area operations with long range, a sprint speed of 470 mph and gross weight of over 21,000 lb.

Right: Another restored airworthy example of the Lockheed twin-boom P-38 Lightning about to take off during a CAF (Confederate Air Force) display.

Below: Hurricane and Thunderbolt, air support for the ground forces in Southeast Asia.

Lockheed P-38 Lightning

Country of origin: USA.

Crew: Fighters, 1; others 2.

Dimensions: Wingspan 15.85 m (52 ft 0 in); length, all fighter versions: 11.53 m (37 ft 10 in); wing area 30.43 m² (327.5 ft²).

Weights: Empty, 5563 kg (12,265 lb); maximum loaded, 8165 kg (18,000 lb).

Engines: Two Allison V-1710 vee-12 liquid-cooled engines driving handed (opposite-rotation) propellers.

Maximum speed: 636 km/h (395 mph).

Service ceiling: 11890 m (39,000 ft).

Range: 1448 km (900 miles) on internal fuel, 2816 km (1,750 miles with drop tanks).

Military load: D: one 37 mm cannon and four 12.7 mm (0.5 in); **E:** cannon changed to 20 mm; **F:** racks added for two tanks, 454 kg (1,000 lb) bombs, torpedo or smoke apparatus; **H, J:** improved M2C cannon and two bombs of 726 kg (1,600 lb).

Above: The Lockheed P-38M, evolved from the P-38L single-seater by adding a second seat (for the radar operator) behind the pilot, and by adding radar in a pod below the nose.

Below: The Lockheed Lightning was perhaps the best twin-engined fighter designed before the Second World War, and reflected Lockheed's great experience in the development of clean aircraft with maximum performance for the given power. Seen here are an F-5B photographic reconnaissance variant (in the foreground) and a standard P-38J fighter.

North American P-51 Mustang

Country of origin: USA.

Crew: 1, though there were 2-seat conversions.

Dimensions: Wingspan 11.278 m (37 ft 0¼ in); length, most: 9.83 m (32 ft 3 in); wing area, most: 21.65 m² (233 ft²).

Weights: Empty, **Mk I, P-51:** 2996 kg (6,605 lb), **D:** 3232 kg (7,125 lb), **H:** 2977 kg (6,563 lb); maximum loaded, **Mk I, P-51:** 3992 kg (8,800 lb), **D:** 5489 kg (12,100 lb), **H:** 5216 kg (11,500 lb)

Engine: One vee-12 liquid-cooled; **I, IA, II, P-51, A, A-36:** 1,150 hp Allison V-1710-F3R

or -39 (some A-36A, 1,325 hp -87); later production models: Packard V-1650 (Merlin), usually 1,520 hp V-1650-3; later **D, K:** 1,590 hp -7, and **H:** 2,218 hp -9.

Military load: I: four 12.7 mm (0.5 in) and four 7.7 mm (0.303 in) Browning machine guns (two 12.7 mm/0.5 in below engine); **II, P-51A:** four 12.7 mm (0.5 in) (in wing); **IA, P-51:** four 20 mm in wing, two 227 kg (500 lb) bombs; **A-36A:** six 12.7 mm (0.5 in) (two below engine), two 227 kg (500 lb) bombs; **B, C** (most): four 12.7 mm (0.5 in), two 454 kg (1,000 lb) bombs; late **B, C,** all **D, K:** six 12.7 mm

(0.5 in), two 454 kg (1,000 lb) bombs, and (D only) six 127 mm (5 in) rockets; **H:** as D.

Above: The most extensively built model of the Mustang was the P-51D, which introduced a one-piece rearward-sliding bubble canopy and, on later models, a small dorsal fin to improve directional stability. Almost indistinguishable was the P-51K, which had an Aeroproducts propeller in place of the Hamilton-Standard unit. Production of the P-51D and P-51K was 7,956 and 1,337 respectively.

Left: Like many of the airworthy Mustangs, this privately owned P-51D based with the Confederate Air Force taking off at Oshkosh in 1978 has been modified to take a passenger seat behind the pilot.

The Grumman F4F Wildcat was built at Trenton, New Jersey in the form of the General Motors FM. The body directly responsible was the Eastern Aircraft Division of GMC, and its ultimate version was the FM-2, which was based on the FM-1 (company designation for the F4F built by Eastern), but had improved features such as a lighter airframe, taller vertical tail and more powerful Wright R-1820-56 Cyclone to maintain performance from smaller carriers, particularly the escort carriers that began to be available from 1942. The F4F/FM type was the only dedicated carrier-borne fighter available to the Allies in 1941 and 1942 able to tackle Axis fighters with any real hope of success. The FM-2 illustrated is part of the Confederate Air Force, based on Rebel Field at Harlingen in Texas, and is painted in the livery of VF-41 'The Red Rippers', located aboard USS *Ranger* in 1941.

Inset: The North American P-51 Mustang has many claims to the title 'best fighter of the Second World War'.

The Hellcat appeared in 1943 as an updated and larger son of the Wildcat, tailored round the 2,000-hp (1,492-kW) Pratt & Whitney R-2800 radial. For a single-seater it was a large aircraft, but it was a match for the Zero in everything except range and agility, and these two factors were improved on later models. But even in its earliest form it was a tough opponent, with excellent protection and firepower. Considerable efforts had been made to keep the structure weight of the Hellcat as low as possible, and this design consideration was taken to the limit with the F8F Bearcat of 1945. This was evolved as an interceptor fighter, and despite being powered by a 2,100-hp (1,567-kW) Pratt & Whitney R-2800-22W Double Wasp radial with water injection for combat boost to 2,800 hp (2,089 kW), it was structurally some 2,287 lb (1,037 kg) lighter than its predecessor. Just too late for the Second World War, the F8F saw limited service in the post-war years.

Below: An Avenger poised for take-off from the American *Ranger* in the Mediterranean

Below: The Vought F4U Corsair was another truly great fighter of the Second World War. It was a massive machine of totally distinct appearance, and was equally at home in combat with Japanese fighters or supporting ground troops with guns, rockets and bombs.

Bottom: Oldest of the famous Grumman 'cat' family is the Wildcat, here represented by an immaculate example based with the Confederate Air Force.

Schemed by Tex Beisel, the F4U Corsair was centred round the use of the most powerful engine currently available, the Pratt & Whitney R-2800 Double Wasp of some 2,000 hp (1,492 kW), to provide the US Navy with a new generation of shipboard fighter with unparalleled performance and versatility. The design was ingenious in the extreme, with a sturdy airframe, considerable internal fuel tankgage, inverted gull wings (to reduce overall span and folded height, and to keep the main landing gear legs short and thus light), and considerable load-carrying capability. Development was protracted by the need for extensive redesign to accommodate extra fuel, but the production F4U-1 entered service late in 1942 as a shore-based fighter, the US Navy having decided that the Corsair's

high landing speed and deck-approach characteristics made it unsuitable for carrier operations. However, the Fleet Air Arm introduced the type into carrier service for relatively small ships, and consequently the US Navy reconsidered its earlier decision.

The Corsair could fight it out with enemy fighters (achieving an 11:1 kill-loss ratio in the Pacific), but achieved its greatest successes as a ground-attack fighter. Gun armament was the standard six 0.5 in (12.7 mm) Browning machine-guns or four 20 mm cannon, and underwing loads could comprise bombs, rockets or extra fuel. In any event the Corsair possessed commendable range, suiting it admirably for operations in the Pacific theatre. The type reached its apogee with the F4U-4, powered by the

2,450 hp (1,828 kW) R-2800-18W radial, bestowing a maximum speed of 446 mph (717 km/h) at 25,000 ft (7,620 m). Armament comprised six 0.5 in (12.7 mm) machine-guns with 400 rounds per gun, plus two 1,000 lb (454 kg) bombs or eight 5 in (12.6 cm) rockets. Facts and figures can do little to convey the significance of this great warplane, which remained in production until 1953, with production reaching 12,571 of all marks. In common with the P-51 Mustang (by then redesignated F-51), the Corsair played an important part in the air operations of the Korean War, its low-level manoeuvrability and offensive load making it one of the best ground-attack machines.

Above left: Curtiss SB2C Helldiver dive-bombers.

Above: The Yokosuka D4Y dive-bomber and reconnaissance aircraft, code-named 'Judy' by the Allies, entered service as a replacement for the Aichi D3A that had proved so devastating a weapon against Allied ships in 1941 and 1942. Like several other types of the Second World War, the D4Y Suisei (comet) was produced in both inline- and radial-engined forms, and was one of the best aircraft operated by the Japanese in the second half of the war.

Below: Super all-rounder – Chance Vought F4U-1D Corsair fighter/strike aircraft aboard USS *Bunker Hill,* 1944.

Top: With aircraft such as the Vought SB2U-1 Vindicator, the US Navy was able to evolve the dive-bombing tactics that stood it in good stead not only for anti-ship operations in the Second World War, but also for the support of US Army and US Marine Corps troops after the Pacific landings that took the Americans back across that ocean for

the final defeat of Japan.

Above: So accurate and devastating was the bombing of aircraft such as the Curtiss SB2C-5 Helldiver in the closing stages of the Second World War that the torpedo-bombing function of machines such as the Grumman Avenger was little used.

Right: This captured Zero fighter, an A6M5 Model 52 of early 1944, typifies the great fighter that was actually an obsolescent and very limited design but which, because of its range and manoeuvrability, and superiority over the even worse collection of aircraft available to oppose it in 1941–43, became synonymous with a myth of Japanese invincibility.

Lower right: The Grumman TBF Avenger first appeared in 1941 and entered service with the US Navy in spring 1942. After a disappointing start it developed into an extremely successful carrier-based torpedo bomber and, with the Royal Navy (initially named Tarpon), it became a general-purpose light bomber, minelayer and strike aircraft. Nearly 10,000 Avengers of various marks were produced, including about 7,000 as TBM-1 and -3, by General Motors.

Below: Douglas SBD-2 Dauntless dive-bombers of Squadron VS-6, based aboard the carrier USS *Lexington*, patrol over the Pacific in October 1941, just before the USA's entry into the Second World War. The US Army also ordered the same basic type under the designation A-24, but then found that dive-bombing was not really suited to its operational requirements.

Grumman TBF and TBM Avenger

Country of origin: USA.

Crew: Usually 3.

Dimensions: Wingspan 16.51 m (54 ft 2 in); length 12.192 m (40 ft 0 in); wing area 45.52 m² (490 ft²).

Weights: Empty, TBF-1: 4572 kg (10,080 lb), TBM-3: 4918 kg (10,842 lb); maximum loaded, TBF-1: 7214 kg (15,905 lb), TBM-3: 8278 kg (18,250 lb).

Range: On internal fuel, both versions approx. 1770 km (1,100 miles).

Engine: Wright R-2600 14-cylinder double-row Cyclone; -1: 1,700 hp R-2600-8; -3: 1,900 hp R-2600-20.

Maximum speed: Both versions: 443 km/h (275 mph).

Service ceiling: 1: 6828 m (22,400 ft); 3: 9174 m (30,100 ft).

Military load: 1: One fixed forward-firing 7.62 mm (0.30 in) (-1C: two 12.7 mm/0.5 in), one 12.7 mm (0.5 in) in turret and one 7.62 mm (0.30 in) ventral; bomb/torpedo load of 726 kg (1,600 lb); -3: two forward-firing 12.7 mm (0.5 in), 12.7 mm (0.5 in) in turret, 7.62 mm (0.30 in) or 12.7 mm (0.5 in) ventral; bomb/torpedo load of 907 kg (2,000 lb).

Left: The Vought SB2U-1 Vindicator was a utility scout and dive-bomber. It was one of the US Navy's first 'modern' monoplanes when it entered service in late 1937. The type had only a short front-line career, but was of considerable importance in the evolution of dive-bombing tactics.

Below: With wings folded, there is little to distinguish the Grumman TBF Avenger from the Grumman fighters apart from its larger size and deep fuselage, with a position for a ventral defensive machine-gun 'stinger'.

The Swordfish was an anachronism, dating from 1932, yet it served throughout World War II, outlasted its intended replacement, and sank a greater tonnage of enemy shipping than any other Allied aircraft. Its forte lay in its load-carrying ability — torpedoes, bombs, rockets, mines — for which it earned the affectionate nickname 'String-bag' when someone observed that 'no housewife on a shopping spree could cram a wider variety of articles into her stringbag'.

Originally known as the Fairey TSR-2 (for torpedo-spotter-reconnaissance), the Swordfish first flew from Great West Aerodrome, on the site of London Heathrow Airport, on 21 March 1933. A total of 2391 was built, virtually all wartime production coming from Blackburn Aircraft's plant at Sherburn-in-Elmet, while Fairey devoted its factory to Albacores, which Blackburn also built. The Swordfish was thus one of very few aeroplanes ever to have been in series production right alongside its successor.

Narvik, Bomba Bay, Cape Matapan, Taranto, North Atlantic, the sinking of the *Bismarck*, campaigns in the Mediterranean and Western Desert — the Swordfish's battle honours are legendary. Its role as a torpedo-bomber ended in 1942 with the catastrophic attempt to prevent the breakout of the German battleships *Gneisenau, Prinz Eugen* and *Scharnhorst* from Brest Harbour. Six of the ancient biplanes, led by Lieutenant-Commander Eugene 'Winkle' Esmonde, were pulverised by the ships' guns in the attack, for which the brave Esmonde was posthumously awarded the Victoria Cross.

Above: The Fairey Firefly carrier fighter/recce aircraft was introduced in 1943 and more than 1,700 were built between then and the end of the 1940s. The Mark 5 Firefly here pictured taking off is the Fleet Air Arm Historic Flight's example finished in the markings of 814 Squadron, with which it started its service life during the Korean War.

Right: Armed with its torpedo, the Swordfish I was remarkably slow, but in some ways this was an advantage, for few anti-aircraft guns of the Second World War were designed to cope with such low speeds.

Top right: Another important World War II aircraft was the Nakajima B5N, which started life as a light bomber during the Japanese invasion of China and was later developed into the B5N1 'Kate' torpedo bomber, 40 of which took part in the Pearl Harbor attack. This B5N2, used mainly on anti-submarine duties in the later stages of the war, has been retouched with Japanese markings for recognition instruction.

Overleaf, page 51: Swordfish in flight.

Top left: A Swordfish comes in to land on the carrier HMS *Emperor*, an escort carrier of the US Navy's 'Sangamon' class, often used for the support of assault landings.

Lower left: Despite its technical obsolescence, the Fairey Swordfish proved an admirable attack aircraft with a torpedo, bombs or rockets.

Above: Blackburn Skua, the Fleet Air Arm's inadequate dive-bomber-cum fighter, in a bombing dive. In the 1940 Norwegian campaign the Skua's success in sinking the light cruiser *Königsberg* was not repeated in the attempt on *Scharnhorst* on 13 June, when 8 out of 15 Skuas were lost.

Right: Bombing-up a Fairey Albacore. Intended as an improved successor to the Swordfish, the Albacore never matched the prowess of the older type, which served with distinction to the end of the war.

Previous page: Albacore torpedo-bombers aboard HMS *Indomitable* in June 1942, having their wings folded before being struck down to the hangar.

Bombers and Attack Aircraft

Bristol Blenheim

Crew: 3.

Dimensions: Wingspan 17.17 m (56 ft 4 in); length, **I:** 12.1 m (39 ft 9 in), **IV:** 12.9 m (42 ft 7 in), **V:** 13.4 m (44 ft 0 in); wing area 43.57 m² (469 ft²).

Weights: Empty, **I:** 3674 kg (8,100 lb), **IV:** 4441 kg (9,790 lb); maximum loaded, **I:** 5670 kg (12,500 lb), **IV:** 6532 kg (14,400 lb), **V:** 7711 kg (17,000 lb).

Engines: Two Bristol Mercury nine-cylinder radials. **Mk I:** 840 hp Mercury VIII, **IV:** 920 hp Mercury XV, **V:** 950 hp Mercury 30.

Maximum speed: I: 455 km/h (283 mph), **IV** early: 472 km/h (293 mph), **IVL:** 429 km/h (266 mph), **V:** 418 km/h (260 mph).

Service ceiling: I, IV: 9000 m (29,500 ft).

Range: I: 1810 km (1,125 miles), **IV:** 2350 km (1,460 miles), **V:** 2575 km (1,600 miles), in each case with bombs and maximum fuel.

Military load: I: 454 kg (1,000 lb) bomb load, fixed 7.7 mm (0.303 in) Browning machine gun in nose, 7.7 mm (0.303 in) Vickers K or Lewis in turret; **IV:** same bomb load plus optional 145 kg (320 lb) external; 7.7 mm (0.303 in) in nose, two 7.7 mm (0.303 in) Browning in dorsal turret and two more in chin turret; **V:** usually as IV.

Early in the war Blenheims attacked the German fleet, served in France and flew many different types of combat mission, and in 1941 made dangerous low-level daylight raids against targets such as Bremen and Cologne. Later in 1941 Blenheims were being replaced in Britain and served increasingly overseas, in Greece, North Africa, Iraq, the Soviet Union, India, Burma and Singapore.

The final model was the Mk V, with an improved dorsal turret, more armour, new nose and more power. In 1942–3 940 were built but by this time the Blenheim was obsolescent and losses were heavy. On one occasion in December 1942 ten Mk Vs went out over Tunisia, met 60 Bf 109s and were almost annihilated, only a single survivor returned. Part of the trouble was that the gross weight had risen by 50 per cent compared with the Mk I, but the main problem was that by 1942 the Blenheim was totally out-of-date.

Right: Vickers Wellingtons of No. 30 Operational Training Unit.

Below: Bristol Blenheim IVL, with long-range fuel tanks in the wings.

Below right: A Fairey Battle prepares to take off from a snow-covered airfield.

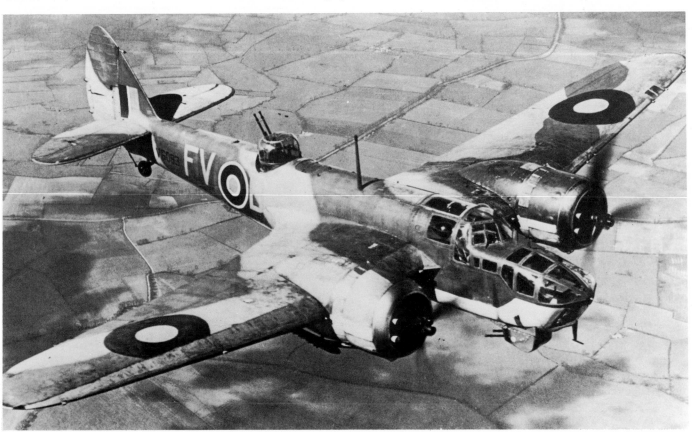

Previous page: The Avro Lancaster may justly be regarded as the epitome of the heavy bomber in the Second World War. Evolved from the unsuccessful Manchester twin-engined bomber, the Lancaster was able to carry the heaviest bombload of any Second World War aircraft, and proved so successful right from the beginning of its career that only minor engine and equipment modifications distinguished the few marks to appear in a massive production programme.

Inset previous page: The Lancaster's forerunner, the Avro Manchester, was the victim of its unsuccessful Vulture engines. This example belonged to No. 207 Squadron.

Below: A Lancaster prepares to take off on a night mission from that familiar wartime location 'somewhere in England'.

Below left: The RAF's first four-engined heavy bomber of the Second World War was the Short Stirling, which was not very successful in its designed role. The RAF had ordained that it must not span more than 100 ft (30.5 m) so as to fit existing hangars, the resulting small wing area entailing a low service ceiling. Seen here is an example of the definitive Mk III heavy bomber version.

Below right: The Armstrong Whitworth Whitley was another of the RAF's new monoplane bombers, entering service in 1937.

Avro Lancaster

Country of origin: Great Britain.

Crew: Normally 7.

Dimensions: Wingspan 31.1 m (102 ft 0 in); length 21.1 m (69 ft 4 in); wing area 119.49 m² (1,297 ft²).

Weights: Empty Mk I: 16705 kg (36,900 lb); maximum gross 30845 kg (68,000 lb); max overload with Grand Slam bomb, 31750 kg (70,000 lb).

Engines: I: Four 1,460 hp Rolls-Royce Merlin 20 or 22 or 1,640 hp Merlin 24 vee-12

liquid-cooled; **II**: four 1,650 hp Bristol Hercules VI 14-cylinder sleeve-valve radials; **III**: four 1,390 hp Packard V-1650 (Merlin 28, 38 or 224).

Service ceiling: (typical) 7467 m (24,500 ft).

Range: Maximum with full bomb-load 2675 km (1,660 miles); with 3175 kg (7,000 lb) bomb-load 4075 km (2,530 miles).

Military load: Normal bomb load 6350 kg (14,000 lb), with

numerous options; defensive armament, tail turret with four 7.7 mm (0.303 in) Browning machine guns (late models sometimes two 12.7 mm/0.5 in); mid-upper turret if fitted two 7.7 mm (0.303 in) (**Mk VII**, two 12.7 mm/0.5 in); nose turret if fitted, two 7.7 mm (0.303 in); Mk II also ventral barbette, two 7.7 mm (0.303 in).

Maximum speed: (all bombers, typical) 462 km/h (287 mph) at 3500 m (11,500 ft).

The 3,429 Mk I aircraft were followed by 3,039 Mk III with Packard Merlins, which usually had broad paddle-blade propellers and with a growing array of radar and ECM equipment. Bomber Command aircraft usually carried the bulky and heavy H_2 mapping radar whose scanner caused a large bulge under the rear fuselage. A small number carried Gee-H precision navigation and 100 Group used many special Lancasters for Elint (electronic reconnaissance), and general counter-measures.

Above: The Handley Page Halifax heavy bomber lacked the glamour of the Lancaster, but was in many respects a finer aircraft. For apart from its nocturnal raids over the Third Reich, the type was also widely used for maritime reconnaissance, anti-submarine work, paratrooping, glider-towing and general transport duties. Seen here is a Halifax II Series 1 on a test flight just after being built.

Left: Ground crews at work on Short Stirlings of No. 149 Squadron at RAF Mildenhall, late 1941. The Stirling was the principal heavy bomber in the early stages of the bombing offensive against Germany.

Above: An outstanding Polish design of the interwar years was the PZL P.23 Karaś (Carp) attack bomber, which entered service in 1935 as an operational trainer and as a reconnaissance bomber in 1936. Over 200 were built for the Polish and Bulgarian Air Forces before Poland was overrun.

Top, right: The most important of the many Henschel designs was the Hs 129 anti-tank/close-support aircraft which first flew in 1939. As the 129B-2/RH it greatly augmented the Ju 87 as a tank destroyer. In this latter role the lean, clean lines evident in this picture were somewhat blurred by a huge ventral pod housing a gun of up to 75 mm calibre.

Right: The Bristol Blenheim I was one of the most advanced types in service when it joined No. 114 Squadron in March 1937.

Overleaf: The Ju 88 had only a small bomb bay, which helped to keep down overall size and weight, and thus to maximise performance. But many types and configurations of disposable weapon load could be carried externally, and here a Ju 88A-5 prepares to take-off with two underwing SC250 551 lb (250 kg) bombs.

Bottom, right: Successor to the effective Savoia-Marchetti S.M.79, the S.M.84 torpedo-bomber adhered to the Italian penchant for the tri-motor configuration, but was not built in large numbers.

Bottom, left: Italy's most powerful bomber of the Second World War was the Piaggio P.108, which entered service only in 1942. Despite a total of 6,000 hp (4,476 kW), which was about the same as the power available to the Lancaster, the P.108 could accommodate only 7,716 lb (3,500 kg) of bombs, and neither range nor speed were particularly impressive. An odd feature, well visible on this P.108B, was the three-deck nose, with the bomb-aimer at the bottom, the nose gunner in the middle and the flight crew at the top.

Left: A unique German attack weapon of the Second World War was the *Mistel* (mistletoe) concept, in which an explosives-packed unpiloted bomber (here a Ju 88A-4) was controlled to its target by a pickaback aircraft (here a Bf 109G fighter). Once the bomber had been aligned to fly into the target, the fighter pilot released his own aircraft and escaped.

Junkers Ju 88

Country of origin: Germany.

Crew: From 2–6 depending on version.

Dimensions: Wingspan A-0 to A-3: 18.36 m (60 ft 2¾ in), all subsequent: 20.0 m (65 ft 7½ in); length, most: 14.39 m (47 ft 2¾ in), G-series with radar and tail-warning: 16.36 m (53 ft 8 in); wing area (except A-0/A-3) 53.5 m² (576 ft²).

Weights: Empty A-1: 7700 kg (16,975 lb), A-4: 9860 kg (21,737 lb); maximum loaded A-1: 10360 kg (22,840 lb), A-4: 14000 kg (30,865 lb), G-7b: 14675 kg (32,353 lb).

Engines: A-1: two Junkers Jumo 211B inverted-vee 12-cylinder, each rated at 1,200 hp; A-4: Jumo 211J of 1,350 hp (also used in many other versions); many C, G and S versions: BMW 801G 18-cylinder radials each rated at 1,730 hp.

Maximum speed: Most, 450 km/h (280 mph), typical S: 610 km/h (379 mph).

Service ceiling: Most, 8000 m (26,250 ft).

Range: Wide variation, but most A-series about 1770 km (1,100 miles).

Heinkel He 111s spearheaded the Blitz which was supposed to soften up Britain for the Nazi invasion. But the lightly armed bombers (Heinkels initially had just three 7.9 mm defensive machine guns, one in the nose and one each at dorsal and ventral positions) proved easy prey for Royal Air Force fighters during the Battle of Britain, and proved beyond doubt to the Luftwaffe high command that speed alone was not sufficient protection in daylight raids.

Despite its failure as a strategic weapon during the Battle of Britain, the Heinkel He 111 was built in ever-increasing numbers. Twice production was halted then resumed again when planned replacements proved unsuccessful, and to the end of the war the old 'Spaten (Spade)' soldiered on, re-engined and re-armed, although the swift heels which it showed to Republican fighters in Spain grew ever slower as the weight of defensive armament, bomb-load and crew went up. Heinkels remained in active service into the late 1960s.

Below: The Junkers Ju 88 has a very good claim to the title of best bomber of the Second World War, and is generally accepted to have been the most versatile aircraft ever built. It was designed as a high-speed medium bomber, and is here seen in the form of the Ju 88S-1, which appeared in the mid-war years with two 1,700-hp (1,268-kW) BMW 801 radials in place of the earlier marks' Junkers Jumo 211 inlines to keep up performance.

Below, inset: An He 111 that has crossed the Atlantic and flies regularly in representative German markings with the CAF (Confederate Air Force) in Texas.

Above: Mosquito bombers with their crews preparing for a mission in February 1943.

Above, right: The Mosquito brought a new level of performance to the job, with a top speed of 380 mph.

Right: Mosquitos proved able to carry out unescorted raids and were used for photographic reconnaissance by the Pathfinder Force. The B.IV was the first bomber variant.

Originally built as a private venture light bomber, the Mosquito was designed to be built entirely of wood, following established De Havilland practice, and with two Merlin engines predicted performance was so good that it was proposed that no armament need be carried. Despite the radical nature of this proposal a small number were ordered, starting with prototype fighter, bomber and photographic reconnaissance versions. The PR versions were the first in service, closely followed by bomber conversions produced while the initial B.IV production bomber variant was awaited. The latter entered service in May 1942 with No 2 Group, and eventually proved able to carry a bomb load of 4000 lb (1814 kg) — compared with a designed load of 1000 lb (454 kg) — over a range of 1450 miles (2335 km). Performance was up to that envisaged, with a top speed of 380 mph (612 km) enabling the type to carry out unescorted daylight raids.

The final approach of the Stuka to the target was made at high level. Once over the target area, the pilot of the Ju 87 half-rolled into a near-vertical dive and plummeted down, his speed held steady by the powerful airbrakes on the wings. The dive from about 14,765 ft (4,500 m) allowed the pilot to line up on the target with extreme accuracy, while the howl of the 'Jericho trumpets' crumbled the resolve of the defence. At about 3,280 ft (1,000 m), reached in about 30 seconds at a dive speed of 348 mph (560 km/h), the pilot pressed the button to initiate the automatic pull-out/bomb-release mechanism, necessary because he might black out during the high-g recovery from the dive. Thus while the elevator was automatically trimmed to pull the aircraft out of its dive, a timer operated the release mechanism for the bomb or bombs. When this had been completed, the pilot resumed control and climbed away from the target.

Below: Stuka, the soubriquet of the Junkers Ju 87 dive-bomber, has become almost synonymous with the concept of ground attack. Seen here is an example of the definitive Ju 87B-1 version, which proved so decisive a weapon in the opening campaigns of Germany's expansion. A single large bomb could be carried on the underfuselage crutch, and four smaller weapons could be accommodated on underwing racks.
Right: The Arado Ar 234 Blitz (Lightning) was the world's first jet bomber when it entered active service with the Luftwaffe early in 1945; a reconnaissance version had been used for several months previously. This first prototype, seen at Rheine in June 1943, used a jettisonable trolley for take-off.

A number of American light bomber types were also used by the RAF in the desert war. The Martin Maryland, like the Douglas Boston, was originally ordered by France, and along with other aircraft in production for the French after May 1940 was taken over by the RAF. The Martin Baltimore was a redesigned Maryland built to RAF specifications, and after early models were delivered with manually aimed Vickers K guns in the dorsal position a Boulton Paul powered turret was installed in the Mk III and a Martin turret in the Mk IV. For close-support work the Baltimore also had a battery of ventral machine guns; two Vickers K guns were standard but some had four or six guns firing downward to the rear as well as four wing-mounted guns, and the bombload of 2,000 lb (907 kg) remained the same as that of the Maryland.

Far left, top: A Martin Baltimore lands at Accra after crossing the Atlantic on its way to join the RAF in the North African desert.

Far left: Martin Maryland attack bombers serving with the Desert Air Force.

Left, above: 500 lb (227 kg) bombs about to be loaded on a Hawker Typhoon IB of No. 175 Squadron, 2nd Tactical Air Force.

Left: A Bristol Beaufort II based on Malta for strikes against Axis shipping in the Mediterranean.

Petlyakov Pe-2

Country of origin: Soviet Union.

Crew: Usually 3.

Dimensions: Wingspan, normal: 17.16 m (56 ft 3½ in), **Pe-21** and other VK-107: 18.0 m (59 ft 0½ in); length, normal: 12.6–12.66 m (41 ft 4¼ in– 41 ft 6 in); wing area 40.5 m² (435.9 ft²).

Weights: Empty, early: 5870 kg (12,941 lb), **M** with PF engines: 5950 kg (13,117 lb); maximum loaded, early: 8496 kg (18,730 lb), late-model **M:** 8520 kg (18,783 lb).

Engines: Two vee-12 liquid-cooled, by Klimov bureau based on Hispano-Suiza design; pre-1943: 1,100 hp M-105R; 1943: 1,260 hp M-105PF (VK-105PF); 1944, some versions: 1,650 hp VK-107A.

Maximum speed: Early, typical: 540 km/h (336 mph); **Pe-2M,** with PF engines: 580 km/h (360 mph); with VK-107A engines: 655 km/h (407 mph).

Service ceiling: All M-105 versions: typically 8800 m (28,870 ft); with 107A engine: 11000 m (36,100 ft).

Range: With bomb load, typical: 1200 km (746 miles); **Pe-2R:** 1700 km (1,056 miles).

Military load: PB-100 and original Pe-2: internal bomb load of 200 kg (441 lb) in fuselage and 100 kg (220 lb) in nacelles, and four 100 kg (220 lb) bombs external; defensive armament of four 7.62 mm (0.30 in) ShKAS, two fixed firing ahead and one aimed above and one below at rear. **Pe-2FT:** upper rear gun replaced by manual UBT turret (with aerodynamic vane to assist rotation) with 12.7 mm (0.5 in) BS; external racks for four 250 kg or two 500 kg (1,102 lb) bombs.

Below: Russia, seeing little need for strategic air operations, produced only one heavy bomber type in the Second World War. This was the Petlyakov Pe-8, which had two unusual features in the provision of gun positions, each with a single 7.62-mm (0.3-in) machine-gun, in the lower part of each inboard engine nacelle, and the use of a fifth engine, located within the fuselage, to power the engine supercharging system.

Right: Though a larger aircraft, the Petlyakov Pe-2 was also an effective attack aircraft, and had much of the versatility of the Ju 88, combining performance with agility and varied weapon loads.

Below: The A-20G was a particularly potent version of the basic A-20/Boston/Havoc/DB-7 series, particularly when it was provided with a twin-gun dorsal turret (A-20G-20 and subsequent blocks). The example illustrated is part of the USAF collection at Dayton, Ohio.

Inset: Shortages of transport aircraft in the Second World War often led to conversions from standard bomber models, as in the case of this Consolidated LB-30 Liberator converted to C-87 standard. This is the oldest Liberator still flying, in the hands of the Confederate Air Force in Texas.

Above: Douglas A-26 Invader attack aircraft support the American drive into Germany during the winter of 1944–45 with bombs dropped round the outer defence zone of the 'Siegfried Line'. Clearly visible in this head-on shot are the Invader's fine liners and heavy forward-firing armament.

Right: The Bristol Beaufighter proved an ideal vehicle for the early airborne interception radar equipment.

Far right: A Martin Marauder, another of the medium bombers to serve with the Allied air forces in the North African and Mediterranean theatres.

The Douglas A-26 Invader was a response to a USAAC requirement for a new-generation attack aircraft, issued in 1940 and calling for a multi-role light bomber able to operate as an attack aircraft at low altitudes, and as a precision light bomber at medium altitudes, with performance parameters requiring high speed, agility and powerful defensive armament. The Invader was pushed rapidly through its development programme and entered service in Europe during 1944. This was a remarkable feat despite the type's clear relationship to the A-20 since the orders for three prototypes (bomber, night-fighter and attack versions) had been placed only in July 1941. The third prototype was selected as the basis for a production order, though it was decided to forego the 75 mm nose-mounted gun that had featured in this model in favour of a nose installation of six 0.5 in (12.7 mm) machine-guns, defence being

underwing hardpoints could carry a further 2,000 lb (907 kg) of bombs, or 16 5-in (12.7 cm) rockets, or eight rockets and two additional fuel tanks. The Invader thus provided the US forces with a new dimension of tactical air support purely from the armament point of view; at the same time the use of two 2,000-hp (1,492-kW) Pratt & Whitney R-2800 radials in an airframe slightly larger and heavier than that of the A-20 series, but somewhat cleaner aerodynamically, provided sparkling performance, including a maximum speed of 355 mph (571 km/h) at 15,000 ft (4,570 m) and a normal range of 1,800 miles (2,896 km). But despite the pace of the Invader's development and early production programmes, only relatively few aircraft saw combat in the Second World War, and large production

entrusted to remotely controlled pairs of 0.5 in (12.7 mm) guns in dorsal and ventral barbettes. But this was only the basis of the gun armament, which could be supplemented by eight more 0.5 in (12.7 mm) guns in four packs under the wings, and two further 0.5 in (12.7 mm) guns in side-mounted blisters on the fuselage nose, giving the devastating forward firepower of 18 0.5 in (12.7 mm) guns as the dorsal barbette could also be locked to fire forwards under the control of the pilot. Internal stowage was provided for 4,000 lb (1,814 kg) of bombs, while contracts were curtailed after the end of hostilities. The A-26, which was redesignated B-26 with the termination of the USAF's A category in 1948, still had an important part to play in future American operations, as events during the Korean War showed.

Right: The military derivative of the L-14 in 1938 was the Hudson maritime patrol bomber developed originally and produced in quantity for the Royal Air Force. The Lockheed Hudson IV (illustrated) is preserved in flying condition by the Strathallan Aircraft Collection in Scotland; it saw action with the Royal Australian Air Force in 1942 and was flown to Scotland from Australia in 1973 for preservation in RAAF markings.

Below: The North American B-25 Mitchell brought a new dimension to the concept of light bombing, for this powerfully armed aircraft (up to 14 0.5 in/12.7 mm machine-guns, sometimes a 75 mm cannon, rocket projectiles and 3,000 lb/1,361 kg of bombs) combined its firepower with good performance to perform more like an attack bomber.

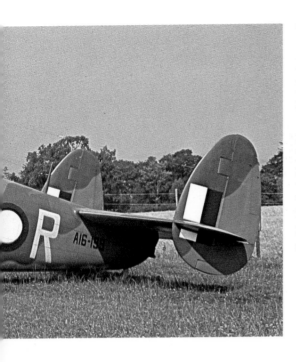

The swing towards the attack bomber was visible in the Baltimore and Tu-2, and fully evident in the US Army Air Force's two classic medium bombers of the war, the North American B-25 Mitchell and the Martin B-26 Marauder. The most numerous of the early Mitchell models was the B-25D, of which 2,290 were built. This featured several improvements introduced successively on earlier models as a result of war experience: power was provided by a pair of 1,700-hp (1,268-kW) Wright R-2600 radials, and armament comprised a bomb-load of 3,000 lb (1,361 kg) carried internally and externally, and six 0.5 in (12.7 mm) machine-guns mounted two each in a fixed nose mounting and power-operated ventral and dorsal turrets. Maximum speed was a creditable 284 mph (457 km/h) at 15,000 ft (4,570 m).

Above: Japan's best bomber of the Second World War was the Mitsubishi G4M, code-named 'Betty' by the Allies. Though classified by the Japanese as a heavy bomber, to the Allies it was a medium bomber with a payload of only 2,205 lb (1,000 kg). Performance was good, but this was achieved only by omitting all types of protection and by making the structure light: as with Japanese fighters, the result was a useful offensive aircraft that could not take the punishment handed out by Allied fighters when the tide turned against Japan.

Top right: A North American Mitchell of No. 28 Squadron, one of the medium bomber squadrons of No. 2 Group, returns from a daylight raid over northern France.

Above: Last and most numerous of the Cant airplanes in the company's 20-year existence was the Z.1007 Alcione (Kingfisher) three-engined bomber, of which over 470 were built. The Alcione had rather light defensive armament and relied on fairly high top speed approaching 300 mph to keep out of trouble.

Right: The tethered stack of B-25 bombers on *Hornet*'s flight-deck, *en route* to her historic Tokyo raid.

85

Upper right: Compared with the B-17E, the B-17F introduced extra fuel and self-sealing oil tanks, and had more guns in an effort to combat German fighters.

Far right: Individual guns were not enough to drive off German fighters, so the Fortresses were operated in boxes for overlapping cones of protective fire.

Right: The chin turret of the B-17G packed a powerful punch, but experienced German pilots still sliced in with their heavy cannon.

Lower far right: The B-17 fleets were the scourge of German industry with precision attacks from high altitude.

Right: Later in the war, fully combat-worthy Flying Fortresses (B-17Fs are seen here) became the mainstay of the US 8th Air Force, which operated from bases in the UK to cut a huge swathe into German fighter and pilot pools.

Below: The B-17 Flying Fortress tore the heart out of Germany's industries and transport systems in the hands of the mighty 8th Air Force. Here an example of the final production series, a B-17G with a chin turret, waits to be bombed up on an English airfield.

Following pages:
Right: Clearly visible on this grounded B-29A are the four-gun forward dorsal turrets designed to deal with the Axis powers' favoured head-on fighter attacks; the twin bomb bays in front of and behind the aircraft's centre of gravity, this requiring the use of an intervalometer to ensure that bombs were released alternately from the forward and after bays; and the tail bumper to ensure that the under-surface of the rear fuselage did not scrape along the runway as the aircraft rotated at take-off.

Left: A trio of B-29s in flight. The natural metal finish was standard after Axis fighter defences declined, higher speed more than compensating for the polished metal's greater glare. The Superfortress nearest the camera is a B-29-BW, the 29th aircraft from a run of 200 that was Boeing Wichita's fourth (out of five) production batch.

Below: A highly-polished B-29A on the tarmac before the installation of its four-gun forward dorsal turret. The use of a four- rather than two-gun turret in this position increased forward-firing gunpower by 50 per cent, to six 0.5 in (12.7 mm) M2 Browning machine-guns.

Above: B-29s of the 39th Bomb Group, 314th Bomb Wing, 20th Air Force (based on Guam), unload their incendiaries over Japan on 16 July 1945.

Below: Superfortresses of the 500th Bomb Group, 73rd Bomb Wing, 20th Air Force, drop unwieldy but terribly efficient fire bombs on Yokohama during a raid on 29 May 1945.

Right: B-29s of the 29th Bomb Group come under attack from a Kawasaki Ki-45 'Nick' heavy fighter. Such a threat was small, for even if the Japanese could get their fighters into the air in time to intercept, the indifferent quality of the pilots made attacks relatively harmless. Additionally, the 'Nick' was some 20 mph (32 km/h) slower than the Superfortress, making interception doubly difficult.

Below: There were losses, however, and here a B-29 heads back towards base with one engine on fire. Radio information from other B-29s, coupled with the presence over the sea of 'Dumbo' and 'Superdumbo' rescue aircraft, meant that the crews of Superfortresses which had to ditch generally faced few survival problems before being picked up by a rescue flying-boat.

The Martin B-26 Marauder was an advanced medium bomber with tricycle landing gear but better performance, provided partially by the type's superb aerodynamic lines and the use of 2,000-hp (1,492-kW) Pratt & Whitney R-2800 radials. Wing area was slightly less than that of the Mitchell, despite a gross weight of 34,200 lb (15,513 kg) in the B-26B compared with 27,100 lb (12,293 kg) for the B-25A, and so low-speed handling characteristics were tricky, resulting in heavy attrition in training. But experience and a slight increase in wing area reduced this steadily, and the B-26 came to possess a combat loss rate to be envied by all. Successive improvements to the type's offensive capabilities resulted in the USAAF's definitive tactical support bomber of the Second World War, the B-26G which served in 1944 and 1945 with enormous distinction. Maximum bombload was 4,000 lb (1,814 kg), and 11 0.5 in (12.7 mm) Browning machine-guns were provided for offence and defence: two were located on each side of the forward fuselage in blisters, two were located in each of the powered dorsal and tail turrets, and three more flexible weapons were disposed to the nose and two beam positions. The importance of the gun armament and additional safety features such as improved armour protection, self-sealing fuel tanks and the like, is attested by the fact that bombload was actually reduced between the B-26B and B-26G models, the 5,200 lb (2,359 kg) of the early model dropping by some 1,200 lb (544 kg) to allow for the protective installations without too great a degradation of performance. The overall

importance in the American armoury of the B-25 and B-26 can be gauged by the types' production, 9,816 and 4,708 respectively.

Sporting the black-and-white 'invasion stripes' of June 1944, a Martin B-26 Marauder of the 386th Bomb Group, US 9th Air Force, unloads six 500 lb (227 kg) bombs over a target in Normandy.